CW00418837

www.booksbyboxer.com

Bee Three Publishing is an imprint of Books By Boxer
Published by
Books By Boxer, Leeds, LS13 4BS UK
Books by Boxer (EU), Dublin D02 P593 IRELAND

MADE IN CHINA
ISBN: 9781915410207

This book is produced from responsibly sourced paper to ensure forest management

Mom Tip:

90% OF PARENTING IS JUST THINKING WHEN YOU CAN GO AND LIE DOWN AGAIN.

Mom Tip:

GIVE NEW MOMS A BLENDER AT THEIR BABY SHOWER.

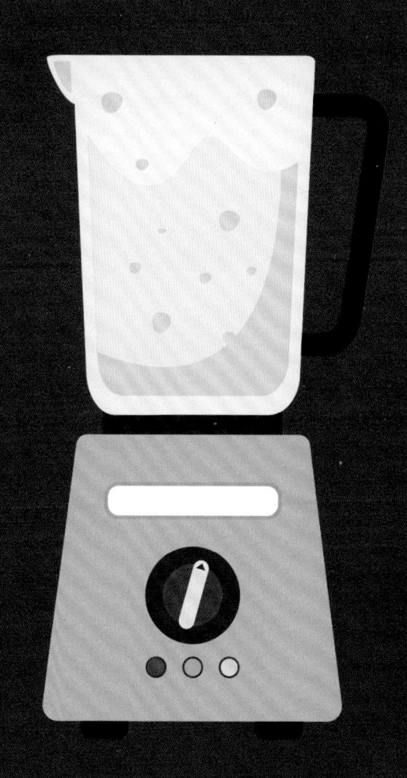

IT DROWNS OUT THE CRYING **AND** MAKES MARGARITAS.

IF YOUR KID ASKS FOR DUCT TAPE, BE AFRAID – THE NEXT 30 MINUTES THAT FOLLOW WILL **NEVER BE GOOD.**

WHEN I TELL MY KIDS I'LL DO SOMETHING IN A MINUTE,

WHAT I'M REALLY SAYING IS **"PLEASE FORGET"**.

Mom Tip:

ENSURE TO TELL THE KIDS THAT ALL YOUR FAVORITE CANDY BARS ARE **SPICY.**

NOW YOU **NEVER** HAVE TO SHARE.

"THE QUICKEST WAY FOR A PARENT TO GET A CHILD'S ATTENTION IS TO SIT DOWN AND BE COMFORTABLE"

- LANE OLINGHOUSE

BEING A PARENT IS LIKE FOLDING A FITTED SHEET, NO ONE REALLY KNOWS HOW.

Mom Tip:

IF YOU DON'T KNOW WHERE YOUR CHILDREN ARE IN THE HOUSE…

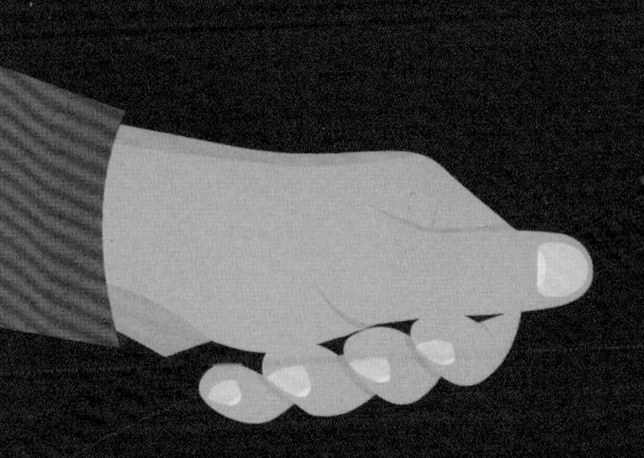

TURN OFF THE INTERNET AND WATCH THEM MAGICALLY APPEAR!

SILENCE IS GOLDEN.
UNLESS YOU HAVE KIDS.
THEN SILENCE IS JUST
SUSPICIOUS.

“HAVING CHILDREN IS LIKE LIVING IN A FRAT HOUSE: NOBODY SLEEPS, EVERYTHING’S BROKEN, AND THERE’S A WHOLE LOT OF THROWING UP.”

– RAY ROMANO

Mom Tip:

IF YOU HAVE TWO KIDS, YOU CAN USE ONE TO GO FETCH THE OTHER WHILE YOU STAY **SEATED ON THE COUCH.**

THIS ALSO WORKS GREAT FOR STAYING IN THE CAR IF IT'S RAINING WHEN PICKING THEM UP FROM A FRIEND'S HOUSE.

"IF YOUR KIDS
ARE GIVING YOU A
HEADACHE, FOLLOW
THE DIRECTIONS
ON THE ASPIRIN
BOTTLE, ESPECIALLY
THE PART THAT SAYS
'**KEEP AWAY FROM
CHILDREN**'."

– SUSAN SAVANNAH

I'M GOING TO STOP BUYING TOYS FOR MY KIDS, BECAUSE THEIR FAVORITE THING TO PLAY WITH IS MY LAST NERVE.

Mom Tip:

NO ONE IN YOUR FAMILY WILL APPRECIATE THAT YOU STAYED UP **ALL NIGHT** OVERTHINKING FOR THEM.

Motherhood:

FEEDING THEM AS A BABY AND THEN THROUGH MOST OF THEIR TWENTIES.

PARENTING IS A CONSTANT BATTLE BETWEEN GOING TO BED TO CATCH UP ON SOME SLEEP OR STAYING AWAKE TO FINALLY GET SOME ALONE TIME.

Mom Tip:

NEED 5 MINUTES OF PEACE? START A GAME OF HIDE AND SEEK... JUST TAKE YOUR TIME FINDING THEM!

"IF EVOLUTION REALLY WORKS, HOW COME MOTHERS ONLY HAVE TWO HANDS?"

– MILTON BERLE

NOBODY LEARNS PARKOUR
FASTER THAN A PARENT
CHASING A TODDLER
WITH A SHARPIE.

Mom Tip:

THE EASIEST WAY TO SHOP WITH KIDS IS **NOT TO.**

I DON'T WANT TO
SLEEP LIKE A BABY.

I WANT TO SLEEP
LIKE MY HUSBAND.

"A TWO-YEAR OLD IS KIND OF LIKE HAVING A BLENDER, BUT YOU DON'T HAVE A TOP FOR IT."

- JERRY SEINFELD

Mom Tip:

ENJOY THE 7 SECONDS AFTER YOU'VE MOPPED THE FLOOR BEFORE IT'S **DISGUSTING AGAIN.**

“MOTHERHOOD IS BASICALLY FINDING ACTIVITIES FOR CHILDREN IN THREE-HOUR POCKETS OF TIME FOR THE REST OF YOUR LIFE.”

– MINDY KALING

I'D LOVE TO BE A PINTEREST PARENT. BUT IT TURNS OUT I'M MORE OF AN AMAZON PRIME PARENT.

Mom Tip:

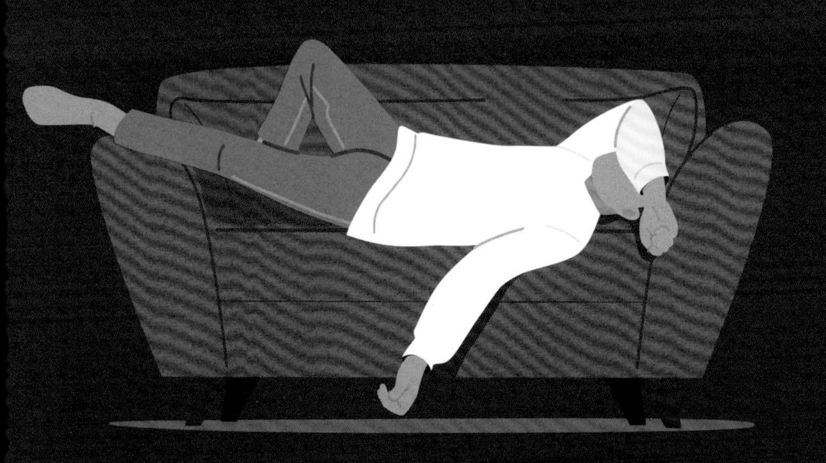

REFRAIN FROM PUNCHING YOUR HUSBAND WHEN YOU TELL THE KIDS IT'S BEDTIME, BUT THEN HE SAYS THEY CAN HAVE 5 MORE MINUTES.

Momster:

WHAT HAPPENS TO A MOM AFTER SHE COUNTS TO 3...

AS A PARENT,
'NETFLIX & CHILL'

MEANS PUTTING ON THE KIDS CHANNEL SO YOU CAN SIT DOWN FOR 10 MINUTES.

Mom Tip:

MAKE SACRIFICES FOR YOUR KIDS...

FOR EXAMPLE; IF YOU EAT THE LAST COOKIE, YOUR KIDS WON'T HAVE TO FIGHT OVER IT.

"WHEN YOUR CHILDREN ARE TEENAGERS, IT'S IMPORTANT TO HAVE A DOG SO THAT **SOMEONE** IN THE HOUSE IS **HAPPY TO SEE YOU."**

– NORA EPHRON

MY KIDS ARE MAKING IT VERY DIFFICULT FOR ME TO BE THE KIND OF PARENT I ALWAYS IMAGINED I WOULD BE.

Mom Tip:

ALWAYS CARRY WIPES.

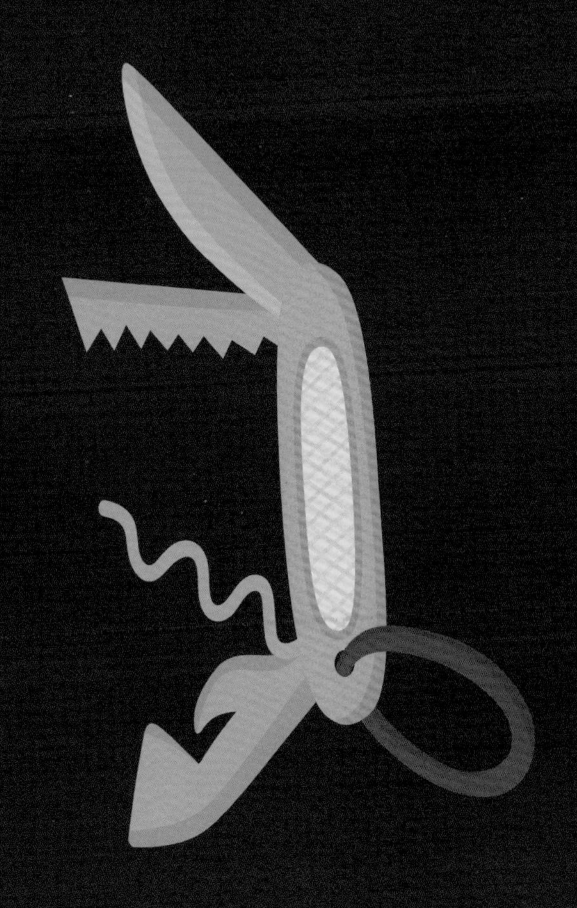

THEY ARE THE SWISS ARMY KNIFE OF PARENTING.

MY CHILD IS TURNING OUT EXACTLY LIKE ME.

WELL PLAYED KARMA, WELL PLAYED.

"THERE IS NO
SUCH THING AS A
PERFECT PARENT.
SO JUST BE A
REAL ONE."

– SUE ATKINS

Mom Tip:

IT WILL TAKE YOUR KIDS 10 MINUTES TO PUT THEIR SHOES ON WHEN YOU ASK THEM, BUT THEY WILL BE ABLE TO UNLOCK YOUR PHONE AND OPEN YOUTUBE IN **10 SECONDS**.

"NO ONE TOLD ME I WOULD BE COMING HOME IN DIAPERS, TOO."

- CHRISSY TEIGEN

WHAT HAPPENS WHEN YOUR KIDS CLEAN THEIR ROOM:

2% CLEANING
28% COMPLAINING
70% PLAYING WITH STUFF THEY JUST FOUND

Mom Tip:

NEED SOMETHING DONE?

TELL YOUR KIDS TO DO THE OPPOSITE.

MAY YOUR COFFEE BE STRONGER THAN YOUR TODDLER.

THE WORST THING ABOUT PARENTING ISN'T DIRTY NAPPIES OR LOSS OF SLEEP. IT'S HAVING WHEELS ON THE BUS STUCK ON REPEAT IN YOUR HEAD.

Mom Tip:

TRY NOT TO LAUGH AT NEW PARENTS WHEN THEY SAY THEY'RE GOING TO LIMIT SCREEN TIME.

"LIKE ALL PARENTS,
MY HUSBAND AND I
JUST DO THE BEST WE
CAN, AND HOLD OUR
BREATH, AND HOPE
WE'VE SET ASIDE
ENOUGH MONEY TO
**PAY FOR OUR KIDS'
THERAPY."**

- MICHELLE PFEIFFER

GREAT PARENTING LIES SOMEWHERE BETWEEN 'DON'T DO THAT' AND 'AH, WHAT THE HELL'.

Mom Tip:

DON'T BOTHER PAYING FOR THAT AEROBICS CLASS.

JUST TRY TO SIT DOWN THEN FEEL THE BURN OF A GYM WORKOUT AS YOU REPEATEDLY GET UP **EVERY 3 SECONDS.**

A SLEEPING CHILD'S
NAP TIME IS THE NEW
HAPPY HOUR.

“THE SCARIEST PARTS OF RAISING TEENAGERS IS REMEMBERING THE STUPID THINGS YOU DID AS A TEENAGER.”

– WHITNEY FLEMING

Mom Tip:

NEED TO GET YOUR KID
TO GO TO BED?

ASK THEM TO CLEAN UP
– THEY WILL SUDDENLY
BE **VERY** TIRED.

"SLEEP, AT THIS
POINT, IS JUST A
CONCEPT, SOMETHING
I'M LOOKING FORWARD
TO INVESTIGATING IN
THE FUTURE."

- AMY POEHLER

THEY SAY IT TAKES A VILLAGE. WHERE CAN I GET DIRECTIONS TO THIS VILLAGE?

Mom Tip:

WHEN YOU'RE A PARENT, A BOOTY CALL IS SOMEONE SHOUTING FROM THE BATHROOM FOR YOU TO COME WIPE THEIR BUTTS.

MY NICKNAME IS MOM,

BUT MY FULL NAME IS MOM MOM MOM MOM MOM MOM MOM.

MY KIDS SURE DO MAKE A LOT OF PLANS FOR PEOPLE WHO CAN'T DRIVE THEMSELVES ANYWHERE.

Mom Tip:

DON'T SHOW YOUR KID A NEW TV SHOW OR MOVIE UNLESS YOU'RE PREPARED TO WATCH IT ON REPEAT FOR THE NEXT **3 YEARS.**

“IT JUST OCCURRED
TO ME THAT THE
MAJORITY OF MY DIET
IS MADE UP OF FOOD
THAT MY KID DIDN’T
FINISH…”

- CARRIE UNDERWOOD

HAVING ONE CHILD MAKES YOU A PARENT. HAVING TWO MAKES YOU A REFEREE. THREE OR MORE? NOW YOU'RE BASICALLY A BOUNCER.

Mom Tip:

YOU CAN HAVE GOOD BLOOD PRESSURE OR YOU CAN TAKE YOUR KIDS TO THE STORE.

YOU CAN'T HAVE BOTH.

THE CLOSEST I GET TO A SPA DAY IS WHEN THE **STEAM FROM THE DISHWASHER** SMACKS ME IN THE FACE.

EVERY TIME I SAY 'NO', MY KID HEARS, 'ASK AGAIN, THEY DIDN'T UNDERSTAND THE QUESTION'.

Mom Tip:

DON'T BELIEVE ANYONE THAT TELLS YOU THAT THEIR KIDS ARE ANGELS.

"INSANITY IS HEREDITARY; YOU GET IT FROM YOUR CHILDREN."

– SAM LEVENSON

ONE DAY I WILL BE THANKFUL THAT MY CHILD IS STRONG WILLED, BUT NOT WHILE I'M WRESTLING THEM IN THE GROCERY STORE.

Mom Tip:

MAKE SURE TO GIVE YOUR PARENTS EXTRA LOVE AS YOUR KID GROWS UP AND YOU REALIZE THEY ARE **EXACTLY** LIKE YOU.

RAISING KIDS IS A WALK IN THE PARK.

JURASSIC PARK.

DEAR KIDS, SORRY I YELLED. IN MY DEFENSE, YOU WERE ACTING LIKE A BUNCH OF PSYCHOS.

Mom Tip:

IF YOU WANT TO NAP WHILE THE KIDS ARE HOME, JUST SAY "WAKE ME UP IN 30 MINUTES SO WE CAN CLEAN THE HOUSE."

THEY WILL **NEVER** WAKE YOU.

"I ALWAYS SAY,
IF YOU AREN'T
YELLING AT YOUR
KIDS, YOU'RE NOT
SPENDING ENOUGH
TIME WITH THEM."

- REESE WITHERSPOON

"SO, I STEPPED AWAY FOR LIKE TWO SECONDS..."

- THE BEGINNING OF EVERY PARENTING HORROR STORY.

Mom Tip:

IT'S NOT YELLING,
IT'S MOTIVATIONAL SPEAKING
FOR PEOPLE WHO DON'T WANT
TO LISTEN.

DEAR MOM,

I GET IT NOW...

MY FRIEND ASKED ME RECENTLY
WHAT THE MOST DIFFICULT
PART OF BEING A PARENT IS...
WITHOUT A SHADOW OF A DOUBT
– IT'S THE KIDS.

Mom Tip:

THE ONLY THING YOU'LL BE THROWING BACK NOW IS A LARGE GLASS OF **WINE**.

"WHY DON'T KIDS
UNDERSTAND THAT
THEIR NAP IS NOT
FOR THEM BUT
FOR US?"

- ALYSON HANNIGAN

I THINK MY PATIENCE IS AT THE BOTTOM OF THIS COFFEE CUP. HANG ON WHILE I FIND IT.

Mom Tip:

FUN DRINKING GAME FOR PARENTS. TAKE A SHOT EVERY TIME YOUR KID WHINES.

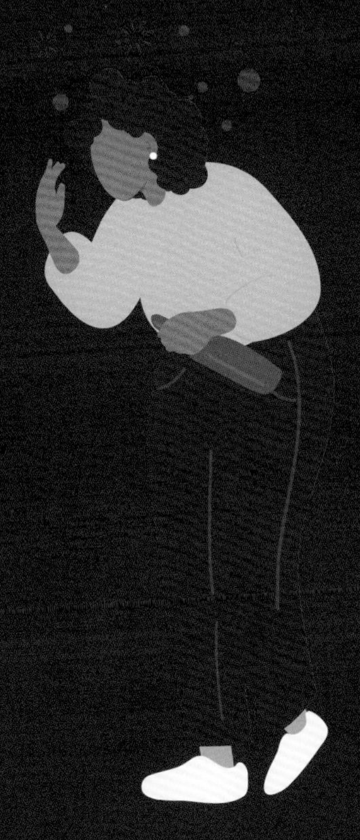

JUST KIDDING, DON'T DO IT.
YOU WON'T SURVIVE.

NOBODY HAS MORE ON THEIR TO DO LIST THAN A TODDLER AT BEDTIME.

"THIS IS GOING TO HURT ME MORE THAN IT HURTS YOU".

EVERY PARENT WHO TAKES AWAY THEIR KIDS' ELECTRONICS.

Mom Tip:

KEEP PUTTING ITEMS ON THE STAIRS FOR YOUR FAMILY TO CARRY UP.

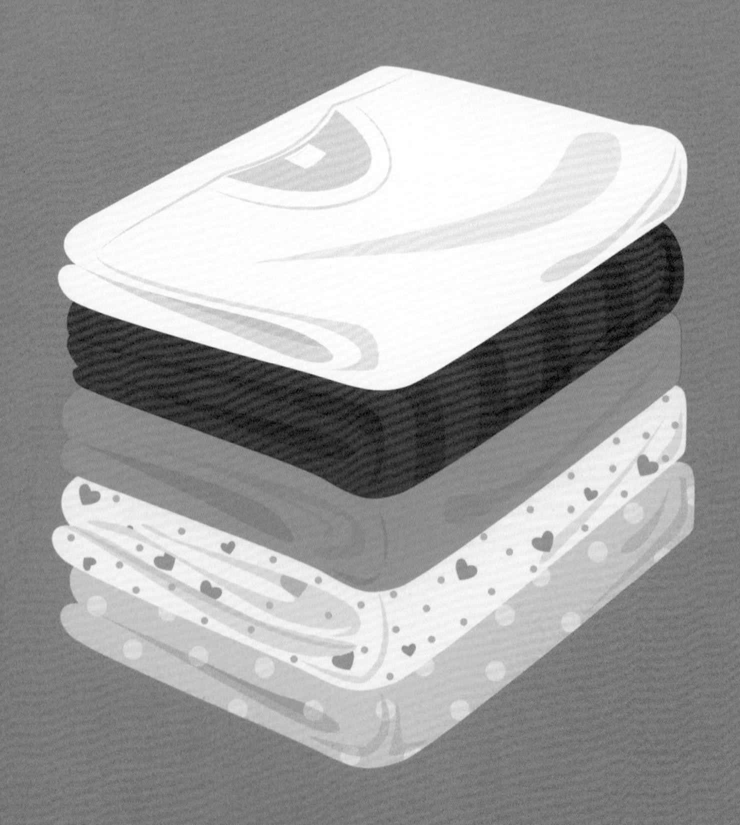

IT PROBABLY WON'T HAPPEN BUT **NEVER LOSE HOPE.**

"IT'S NOT EASY BEING A MOM. IF IT WERE EASY, FATHERS WOULD DO IT."

- BETTY WHITE

SUCCESS IS GETTING THROUGH A DAY WITHOUT ANY STAINS ON YOUR CLOTHES.

Mom Tip:

US PARENTS LIVE FOR TINY VACATIONS FROM OUR KIDS.

LIKE WHEN YOU PUT YOUR KIDS IN THE CAR AND CLOSE THE DOOR. THAT WALK, IT'S WHAT WE CALL A **TINY PARENT VACATION.**

RECIPE FOR
ICED COFFEE:

1. HAVE KIDS.
2. MAKE COFFEE.
3. FORGET YOU MADE COFFEE.
4. DRINK IT COLD.

MY KID JUST THREATENED NOT TO TALK TO ME FOR THE REST OF THE DAY. I'M 3% OFFENDED AND 97% HOPING THEY FOLLOW THROUGH.

Mom Tip:

DON'T SELL YOUR KIDS
ON EBAY.

THEY'RE HANDMADE, YOU COULD
GET A **MUCH** HIGHER PRICE
ON ETSY.

"BECOMING A MOM,
TO ME, MEANS YOU
HAVE ACCEPTED
THAT FOR THE NEXT
16 YEARS OF YOUR
LIFE, YOU WILL
HAVE A STICKY
PURSE."

– NIA VARDALOS

PARENTING STYLE:

SURVIVALIST.

Mom Tip:

IT'S NOT APPROPRIATE TO LAUGH WHEN YOUR KID TRIPS OVER THE TOY YOU ASKED THEM TO PICK UP **100 TIMES TODAY.**

CURRENTLY APPROVING
MY KIDS FRIENDS
BASED ON WHICH
PARENTS I THINK WILL
DRINK WINE WITH ME
ON PLAY DATES.

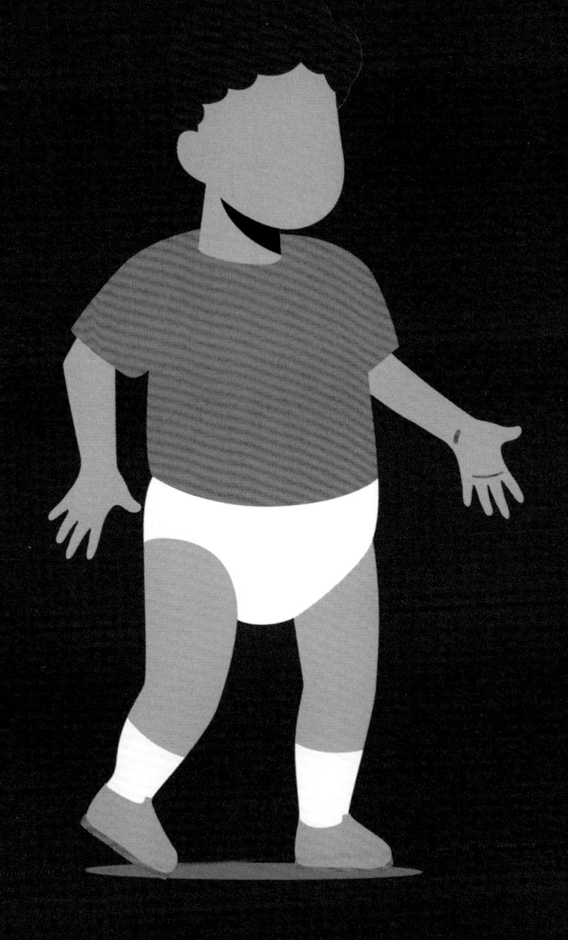

BEFORE I BECAME A PARENT,
I DIDN'T KNOW I COULD RUIN
SOMEONE'S DAY BY ASKING THEM
TO PUT PANTS ON.

Mom Tip:

DON'T MAKE EYE CONTACT WHEN CHECKING ON YOUR CHILD AS THEY GO TO BED OR START TO STIR FROM A NAP.

THEY CAN SENSE FEAR.

"A MOTHER NEED ONLY STEP INTO THE SHOWER TO BE INSTANTLY REASSURED SHE IS **INDISPENSABLE** TO EVERY MEMBER OF HER FAMILY."

- LYNNE WILLIAMS

A GOOD WAY TO PREPARE YOURSELF FOR PARENTHOOD IS TO TALK TO ROCKS, BECAUSE THEY HAVE SIMILAR LISTENING HABITS.

Mom Tip:

THE ONLY WAY TO GET A DECENT PICTURE OF YOUR KIDS IS TO PRETEND YOU ARE NOT IN FACT TAKING A PICTURE.

MY HOUSE LOOKS LIKE
I'M LOSING A GAME
OF JUMANJI.

HELL HATH NO FURY LIKE A CHILD WHOSE SIBLING JUST PRESSED THE ELEVATOR BUTTON.

Mom Tip:

LOST A COFFEE?

TRY THE MICROWAVE, YOU PROBABLY LEFT IT THERE THE LAST TIME YOU TRIED TO REHEAT IT.

"WINE IS NECESSARY."

– KELLY CLARKSON

I CHILDPROOFED MY ENTIRE HOUSE - BUT SOMEHOW THEY STILL KEEP GETTING IN!

Mom Tip:

DON'T YELL AT YOUR KIDS.

LEAN IN AND WHISPER,
IT'S MUCH SCARIER.

I LOVE CLEANING UP MESSES I DIDN'T MAKE.
SO I BECAME A MOM.

BUT MOM WHAT IF I GET KIDNAPPED?

TRUST ME, THEY WILL BRING YOU BACK.

Mom Tip:

JUST BECAUSE YOUR KID
ATE 3 BANANAS YESTERDAY,
DOESN'T MEAN THEY WILL
LIKE THEM TODAY.

“CHILDREN ARE LIKE CRAZY, DRUNKEN SMALL PEOPLE IN YOUR HOUSE.”

- JULIE BOWEN

CLEANING WITH A TODDLER IS LIKE RAKING LEAVES DURING A HURRICANE.

Mom Tip:

DON'T BOTHER BUYING AN ALARM CLOCK ONCE YOU HAVE KIDS.

BASED ON THE AMOUNT OF LAUNDRY I HAVE TO DO ON A DAILY BASIS; I'M GOING TO ASSUME THERE ARE PEOPLE LIVING IN THIS HOUSE THAT **I HAVEN'T MET YET.**

CHILDREN REMIND US ALL OF THE PRECIOUS THINGS IN LIFE, LIKE UNINTERRUPTED SLEEP, EXTRA SPENDING MONEY AND SANITY.

Mom Tip:

ONLY ONE OF THESE THINGS CAN LOOK GOOD AT **ANY** GIVEN TIME: YOU, THE KIDS, OR THE HOUSE.

"THERE ARE THREE
WAYS TO GET
SOMETHING DONE: DO
IT YOURSELF, HIRE
SOMEONE TO DO IT,
OR ASK YOUR KIDS
NOT TO DO IT."

– MALCOLM KUSHNER

BOYS: LESS DRAMA THAN GIRLS, BUT A LOT HARDER TO KEEP ALIVE.

Mom Tip:

THE WEEKENDS USED TO BE FOR DRINKING, NOW THEY ARE FOR 15 LOADS OF LAUNDRY.

MOMS, INSTEAD OF JUDGING EACH OTHER, LET'S SUPPORT EACH OTHER LIKE WE USED TO WHEN WE WERE **DRUNK** IN THE **CLUB BATHROOMS.**

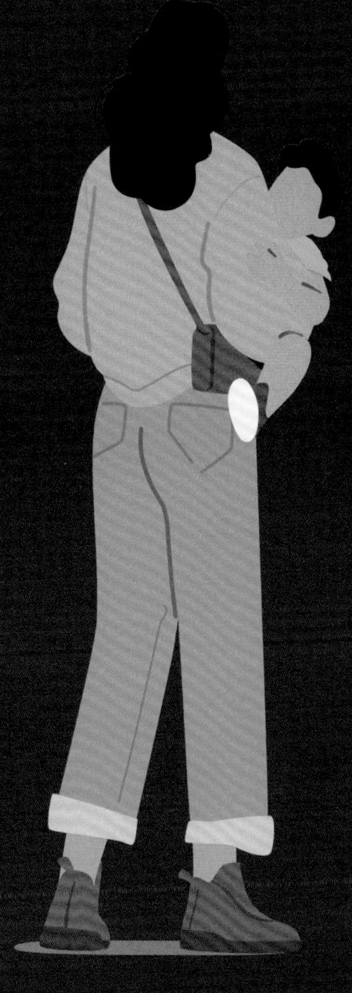

PARENTHOOD IS JUST ONE LONG HOSTAGE SITUATION, EXCEPT THERE'S NOBODY COMING TO SAVE YOU.

Mom Tip:

AS SOON AS YOU THINK YOU'VE CRACKED PARENTING, THEY WILL GROW INTO A WHOLE NEW STAGE OF **WTF**.

"WAKING YOUR KIDS
UP FOR SCHOOL THE
FIRST DAY AFTER A
BREAK IS ALMOST
AS MUCH FUN AS
BIRTHING THEM WAS."

- JENNY MCCARTHY

WHEN YOUR MOM VOICE IS SO LOUD EVEN YOUR NEIGHBORS BRUSH THEIR TEETH AND GET DRESSED.

Mom Tip:

MOTHERHOOD IS AN EXTREME SPORT.

IT'S THE REAL REASON FOR WORKOUT CLOTHES.

IF I EVER GO MISSING,
PLEASE FOLLOW MY KIDS.
THEY CAN FIND ME NO MATTER
WHERE I **TRY TO HIDE.**

"THERE'S NO WAY
TO BE A PERFECT
MOTHER AND A
MILLION WAYS TO BE
A GOOD ONE."

- JILL CHURCHILL

Mom Tip:

WHENEVER YOU FEEL LIKE A BAD PARENT, REMEMBER THAT THE MOM FROM HOME ALONE WAS HALFWAY TO PARIS BEFORE SHE REALIZED SHE WAS **MISSING A CHILD.**

"RAISING A KID IS PART JOY AND PART GUERILLA WARFARE."

- ED ASNER

BECOMING A MOTHER MAKES YOU REALIZE THAT YOU CAN DO ALMOST ANYTHING ONE-HANDED.

Mom Tip:

A PILE OF UNFOLDED LAUNDRY IS GREAT FOR A SECRET **NAP SPOT.**

EVEN BETTER IF THE LAUNDRY IS FRESH FROM THE DRYER AND STILL WARM.

MOST OF MY TIME AS A MOTHER HAS BEEN SPENT IN A CLOSET, EATING SOMETHING I **DIDN'T WANT TO SHARE.**

THE ONLY SHIFT AVAILABLE IN
MOTHERHOOD IS 24/7.

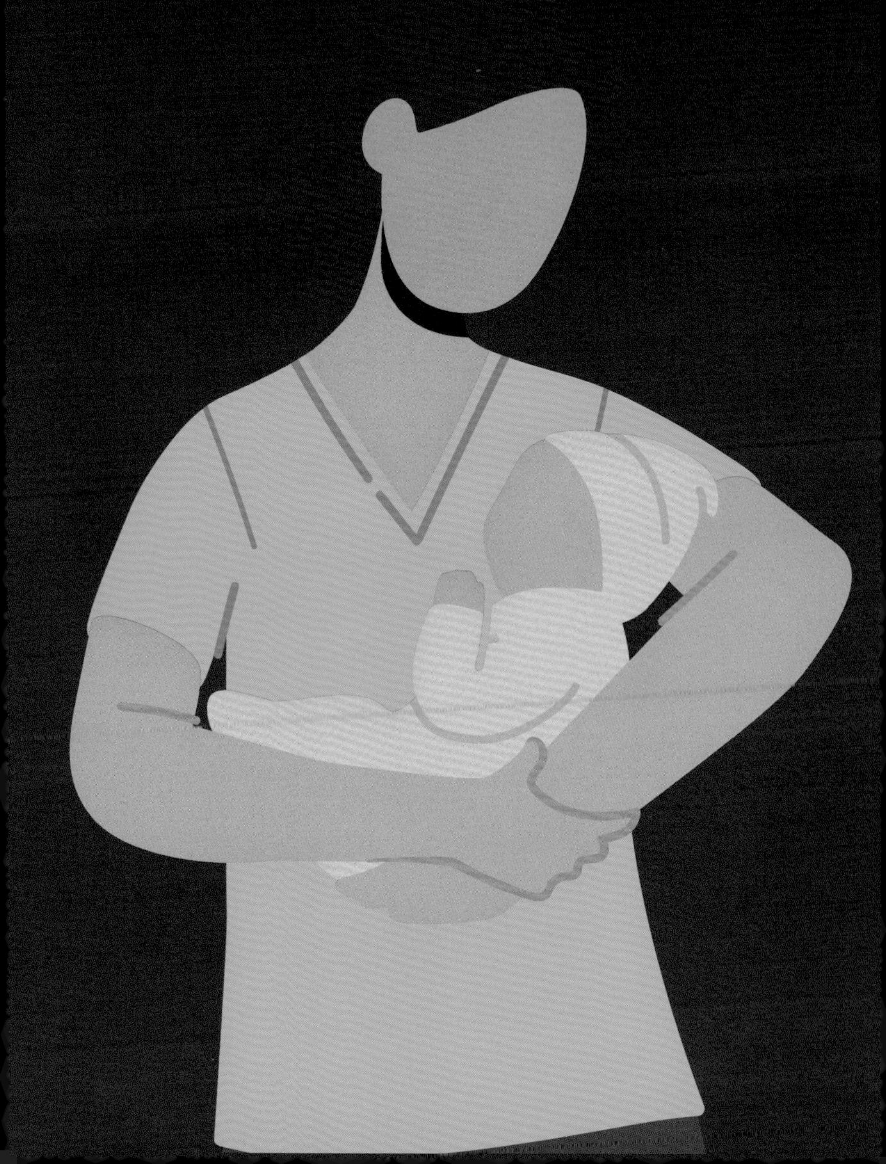

Mom Tip:

DON'T START ELF ON THE SHELF… IT'S A GAME THAT WILL NEVER END.

"ONLY I CAN UNDERSTAND MY KID. SHE'S LIKE 'BDIDKDKODKD JXUDHEJSLOSJDHDU JMSOZUZUSJSIXOJ' AND I'M LIKE, 'OK, I WILL GET YOU A PIECE OF SAUSAGE IN JUST A MINUTE.'"

- CHRISSY TEIGEN

Parenting Hack:

THERE ARE NO HACKS. THERE IS NO WAY TO MAKE YOUR KIDS LISTEN. GOOD LUCK.

Mom Tip:

IF YOUR KID STARTS A MELTDOWN IN PUBLIC - START CRYING LOUDER AND HARDER.

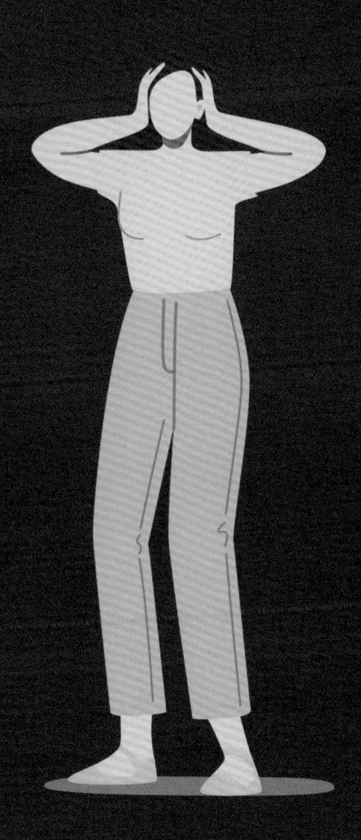

THE **EMBARRASSMENT** WILL STOP THEIR CRYING.

'YOU'RE NOT THE BOSS OF ME',
I WHISPER UNDER MY BREATH,
AS I MAKE 4 DIFFERENT
LUNCHES FOR MY KIDS.

REMEMBER WHEN YOU THOUGHT YOU WERE TIRED BACK BEFORE YOU HAD KIDS?

NOW YOU **REALLY** KNOW WHAT TIRED FEELS LIKE!

Mom Tip:

CHILDREN ARE A GREAT EXCUSE WHEN YOU DON'T WANT TO GO SOMEWHERE WHEN INVITED.

E.G. SORRY, CASEY ISN'T FEELING WELL TODAY, MAYBE NEXT TIME.

"HAVING A BABY IS JUST
LIVING IN THE CONSTANT
UNEXPECTED. YOU NEVER
KNOW WHEN YOU'RE GONNA
GET CRAPPED ON OR WHEN
YOU'RE GONNA GET A BIG
SMILE OR WHEN THAT
SMILE IMMEDIATELY TURNS
INTO HYSTERICS. IT
MIGHT BE LIKE LIVING
WITH A **DRUG ADDICT.**"

- BLAKE LIVELY

IF YOU STEAL MY IDENTITY, YOU BEST BELIEVE IT ALSO COMES WITH MY KIDS. PLEASE – TAKE THEM!

Mom Tip:

KIDS ARE **GREAT PROBLEM SOLVERS.** GIVE THEM A BASKET FULL OF ODD SOCKS AND GET THEM TO PAIR THEM UP...

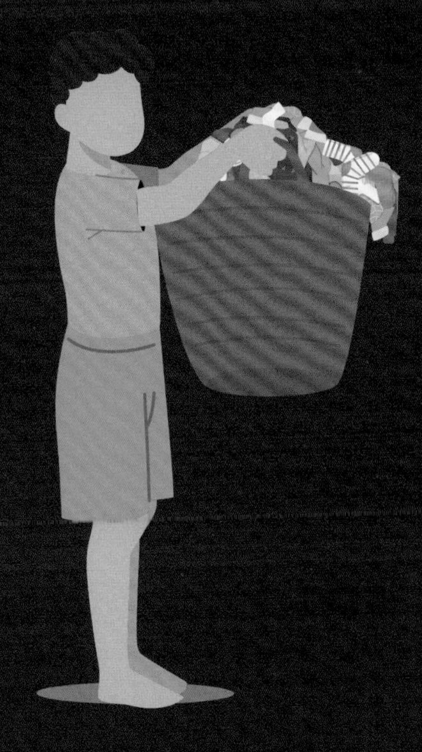

WHILE YOU ENJOY SOME PEACE AND QUIET!

WHEN YOU TRY TO MAKE PLANS WITH OTHER MOM FRIENDS AND YOU REALIZE NONE OF YOU ARE FREE FOR THE NEXT **20 YEARS.**

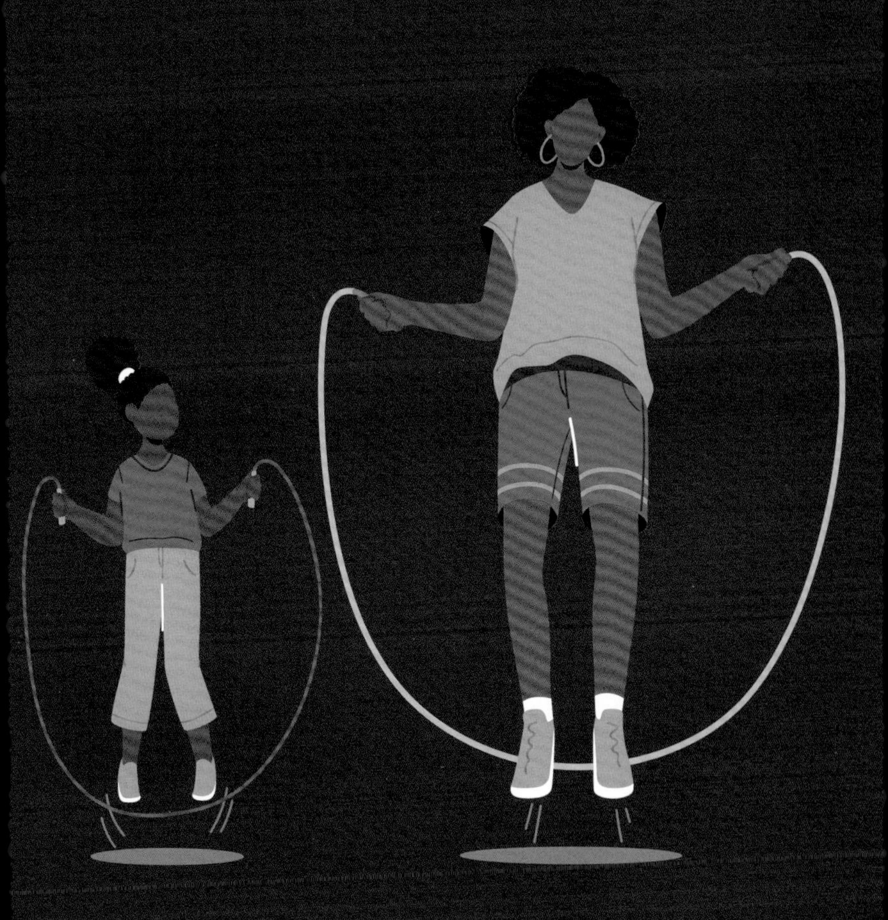

SHOUTOUT TO THE PARENT WHO STEPS UP AND PLAYS WITH THE KIDS SO THE REST OF US CAN TALK IN PEACE.

Mom Tip:

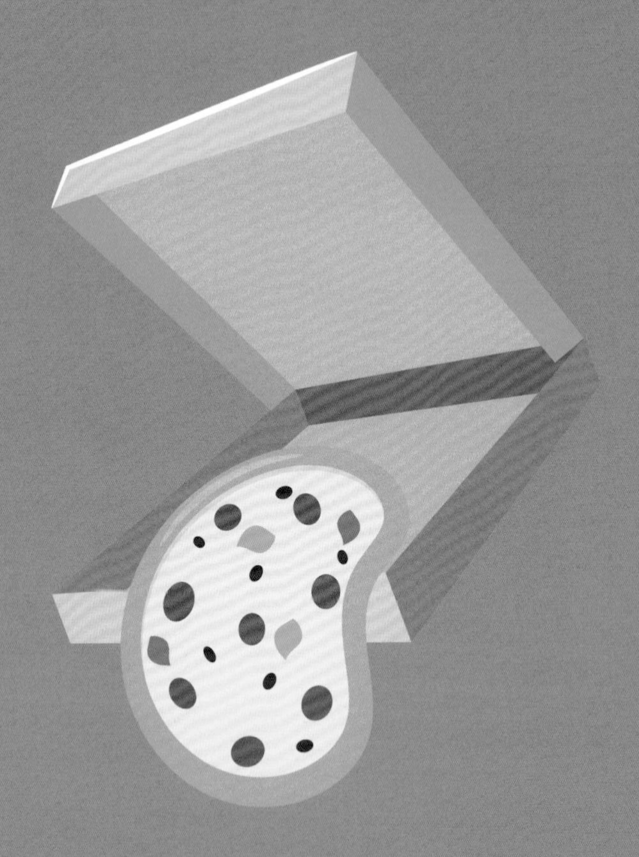

IF YOUR KIDS INSIST ON MAKING YOU DINNER, **IT'S NOT WORTH IT.** JUST CAVE AND GET TAKE OUT, THEN AT LEAST EVERYONE IS HAPPY.

"ANY MOTHER COULD PERFORM THE JOBS OF SEVERAL AIR-TRAFFIC CONTROLLERS WITH EASE."

- LISA ALTHER

'WELL – THAT ESCALATED QUICKLY' IS PRETTY MUCH OUR LIFE'S MOTTO AT THIS POINT.

Mom Tip:

TRAIN YOUR KIDS TO CATCH **ALL THE SPIDERS**, EVEN IF YOU ARE SCARED OF THEM, AND SOON THEY CAN BE THE ONES WHO CATCH THEM!

HOW TO KEEP UP WITH LAUNDRY:
1. YOU CAN'T.
2. FIND A NEW DREAM.

DON'T COMPARE YOURSELF TO OTHER PARENTS. EVERYONE IS LOSING THEIR MIND SLOWLY, SOME ARE JUST BETTER AT HIDING IT THAN OTHERS...

Mom Tip:

IF YOU DON'T WANT TO GIVE YOUR KIDS YOUR FOOD, JUST TELL THEM IT'S **MADE FROM BROCCOLI!**